THE GODS

A LECTURE

by
Robert G. Ingersoll

"AN HONEST GOD IS THE NOBLEST WORK OF MAN"

THE BOOK TREE
San Diego, California

Originally published
1910
by C. P. Farrell
New York
All Rights Reserved

New material, revisions and cover
© by The Book Tree 2010

ISBN 978-1-58509-316-8

Cover layout & design
Atulya Berube

Published by
The Book Tree
P.O. Box 16476
San Diego, CA 92176
www.thebooktree.com

We provide fascinating and educational products to help awaken the public to new ideas and information that would not be available otherwise.
Call 1 (800) 700-8733 for our *FREE BOOK TREE CATALOG*.

TO

EVA A. INGERSOLL,

MY WIFE,

A WOMAN WITHOUT SUPERSTITION,

THIS VOLUME

IS DEDICATED.

INTRODUCTION

Every culture has its gods. These gods are looked upon to lead the way in our moral and spiritual development. But every culture has failed to reach an acceptable level of moral or spiritual development in part, because of these gods.

The problem, according to Ingersoll, is that the gods of man were made by man. They originally appeared within our flawed minds, and therefore resemble their flawed creators. They cannot "rescue" us when they, like us, are in a constant battle for recognition and supremacy, either among themselves or with the gods of other religions.

This book will make you think about the nature of deity and will challenge your critical thinking skills. For example, Ingersoll asks, If an infinite universe has been made out of an infinite god, how much of the god is left?

Heaven is also an issue. The author states that if heaven exists then those who reside there are obviously too happy to have sympathy and help a suffering world. They are too busy singing and enjoying paradise to help the distressed. In this book the author continually brings to our attention the nagging feeling that something is not right, especially as it relates to what we have been traditionally taught. Many of the author's arguments are strong and compelling, while others may be challenged and debated through deeper examination. Whatever the case, this is a insightful book that is well worth exploring.

Paul Tice

FOR THE LOVE OF GOD.

FOR THE USE OF MAN.

THE GODS.

An Honest God is the Noblest Work of Man.

EACH nation has created a god, and the god has always resembled his creators. He hated and loved what they hated and loved, and he was invariably found on the side of those in power. Each god was intensely patriotic, and detested all nations but his own. All these gods demanded praise, flattery, and worship. Most of them were pleased with sacrifice, and the smell of innocent blood has ever been considered a divine perfume. All these gods have insisted upon having a vast number of priests, and the priests have always insisted upon being supported by the people, and the principal business of these priests has been to boast about their god, and to insist that he could easily vanquish all the other gods put together.

These gods have been manufactured after numberless models, and according to the most grotesque fashions. Some have a thousand arms, some a hundred heads, some are adorned with necklaces of living snakes, some are armed with clubs, some with sword and shield, some with bucklers, and some have wings as a cherub; some were invisible, some would show themselves entire, and some would only show their backs; some were jealous, some were foolish, some turned themselves into men, some into swans, some into bulls, some into doves, and some into Holy Ghosts, and made love to the beautiful daughters of men. Some were married — all ought to have been — and some were considered as old bachelors from all eternity. Some had children, and the children were turned into gods and worshiped as their fathers had been. Most of these gods were revengeful, savage, lustful, and ignorant. As they generally depended upon their priests for information, their ignorance can hardly excite our astonishment.

These gods did not even know the shape of the worlds they had created, but supposed them perfectly flat. Some thought the day could be lengthened by stopping the sun, that the blowing of horns could throw down the walls of a city, and all knew so little of the real nature of the people they had created, that they commanded the people to love them. Some were so ignorant as to suppose that man could believe just as he might desire, or as they might command, and that to be governed by observation, reason, and experience was a most foul and damning sin. None of these gods could give a true account of the creation of this little earth. All were wofully deficient in geology and astronomy. As a rule, they were most miserable legislators, and as executives, they were far inferior to the average of American presidents.

These deities have demanded the most abject and degrading obedience. In order to please them, man must lay his very face in the dust. Of course, they have always been partial to the people who created them, and have generally shown their partiality by assisting those people to rob and destroy others, and to ravish their wives and daughters.

Nothing is so pleasing to these gods as the butchery of unbelievers. Nothing so enrages them, even now, as to have some one deny their existence.

Few nations have been so poor as to have but one god. Gods were made so easily, and the raw material cost so little, that generally the god market was fairly glutted, and heaven crammed with these phantoms. These gods not only attended to the skies, but were supposed to interfere in all the affairs of men. They presided over everybody and everything. They attended to every department. All was supposed to be under their immediate control. Nothing was too small — nothing too large; the falling of sparrows and the motions of the planets were alike attended to by these industrious and observing deities. From their starry thrones they frequently came to the earth for the purpose of imparting information to man. It is related of one that he came amid thunderings and lightnings in order to tell the people that they should not cook a kid in its mother's milk. Some left their shining abodes to tell women that they should, or should not, have children, to inform a priest how to cut and wear his apron, and to give directions as to the proper manner of cleaning the intestines of a bird.

When the people failed to worship one of these gods, or failed to feed and clothe his priests, (which was much the same thing,) he generally visited them with pestilence and famine. Sometimes he allowed some other nation to drag them into slavery—to sell their wives and children; but generally he glutted his vengeance by murdering their first-born. The priests always did their whole duty, not only in predicting these calamities, but in proving, when they did happen, that they were brought upon the people because they had not given quite enough to them.

These gods differed just as the nations differed; the greatest and most powerful had the most powerful gods, while the weaker ones were obliged to content themselves with the very off-scourings of the heavens. Each of these gods promised happiness here and hereafter to all his slaves, and threatened to eternally punish all who either disbelieved in his existence or suspected that some other god might be his superior; but to deny the existence of all gods was, and is, the crime of crimes. Redden your hands with human blood; blast by slander the fair fame of the innocent; strangle the smiling child upon its mother's knees; deceive, ruin and desert the beautiful girl who loves and trusts you, and your case is not hopeless. For all this, and for all these you may be forgiven. For all this, and for all these, that bankrupt court established by the gospel, will give you a discharge; but deny the existence of these divine ghosts, of these gods, and the sweet and tearful face of Mercy becomes livid with eternal hate. Heaven's golden gates are shut, and you, with an infinite curse ringing in your ears, with the brand of infamy upon your brow, commence your endless wanderings in the lurid gloom of hell — an immortal vagrant — an eternal outcast — a deathless convict.

One of these gods, and one who demands our love, our admiration and our worship, and one who is worshiped, if mere heartless ceremony is worship, gave to his chosen people for their guidance, the following laws of war: "When thou comest nigh unto a city to fight against it, *then proclaim peace unto it.* And it shall be if it make thee answer of peace, and open unto thee, then it shall be that all the people that is found therein shall be tributaries unto thee, and they shall serve thee. And if it will make no peace with thee, but will make war against thee, then thou shalt besiege it.

And when the Lord thy God hath delivered it into thy hands, thou shalt smite every male thereof with the edge of the sword. But the women and the little ones, and the cattle, and all that is in the city, even all the spoil thereof, shalt thou take unto thyself, and thou shalt eat the spoil of thine enemies which the Lord thy God hath given thee. Thus shalt thou do unto all the cities which are very far off from thee, which are not of the cities of these nations. But of the cities of these people which the Lord thy God doth give thee for an inheritance, *thou shalt save alive nothing that breatheth.*"

Is it possible for man to conceive of anything more perfectly infamous? Can you believe that such directions were given by any being except an infinite fiend? Remember that the army receiving these instructions was one of invasion. Peace was offered upon condition that the people submitting should be the slaves of the invader; but if any should have the courage to defend their homes, to fight for the love of wife and child, then the sword was to spare none — not even the prattling, dimpled babe.

And we are called upon to worship such a God; to get upon our knees and tell him that he is good, that he is merciful, that he is just, that he is love. We are asked to stifle every noble sentiment of the soul, and to trample under foot all the sweet charities of the heart. Because we refuse to stultify ourselves—refuse to become liars—we are denounced, hated, traduced and ostracized here, and this same god threatens to torment us in eternal fire the moment death allows him to fiercely clutch our naked helpless souls. Let the people hate, let the god threaten—we will educate them, and we will despise and defy him.

The book, called the Bible, is filled with passages equally horrible, unjust and atrocious. This is the book to be read in schools in order to make our children loving, kind and gentle! This is the book to be recognized in our Constitution as the source of all authority and justice!

Strange! that no one has ever been persecuted by the church for believing God bad, while hundreds of millions have been destroyed for thinking him good. The orthodox church never will forgive the Universalist for saying "God is love." It has always been considered as one of the very highest evidences of true and undefiled religion to insist that all men, women and children deserve eternal damnation. It has always been heresy to say, "God will at last save all."

We are asked to justify these frightful passages, these infamous laws of war, because the Bible is the word of God. As a matter of fact, there never was, and there never can be, an argument, even tending to prove the inspiration of any book whatever. In the absence of positive evidence, analogy and experience, argument is simply impossible, and at the very best, can amount only to a useless agitation of the air. The instant we admit that a book is too sacred to be doubted, or even reasoned about, we are mental serfs. It is infinitely absurd to suppose that a god would address a communication to intelligent beings, and yet make it a crime, to be punished in eternal flames, for them to use their intelligence for the purpose of understanding his communication. If we have the right to use our reason, we certainly have the right to act in accordance with it, and no god can have the right to punish us for such action.

The doctrine that future happiness depends upon belief is monstrous. It is the infamy of infamies. The notion that faith in Christ is to be rewarded by an eternity of bliss, while a dependence upon reason, observation, and experience merits everlasting pain, is too absurd for refutation, and can be relieved only by that unhappy mixture of insanity and ignorance, called "faith." What man, who ever thinks, can believe that blood can appease God? And yet, our entire system of religion is based upon that belief. The Jews pacified Jehovah with the blood of animals, and according to the Christian system, the blood of Jesus softened the heart of God a little, and rendered possible the salvation of a fortunate few. It is hard to conceive how the human mind can give assent to such terrible ideas, or how any sane man can read the Bible and still believe in the doctrine of inspiration.

Whether the Bible is true or false, is of no consequence in comparison with the mental freedom of the race.

Salvation through slavery is worthless. Salvation from slavery is inestimable.

As long as man believes the Bible to be infallible, that book is his master. The civilization of this century is not the child of faith, but of unbelief—the result of free thought.

THE GODS.

All that is necessary, as it seems to me, to convince any reasonable person that the Bible is simply and purely of human invention — of barbarian invention — is to read it. Read it as you would any other book; think of it as you would of any other; get the bandage of reverence from your eyes; drive from your heart the phantom of fear; push from the throne of your brain the cowled form of superstition—then read the Holy Bible, and you will be amazed that you ever, for one moment, supposed a being of infinite wisdom, goodness and purity, to be the author of such ignorance and of such atrocity.

Our ancestors not only had their god-factories, but they made devils as well. These devils were generally disgraced and fallen gods. Some had headed unsuccessful revolts; some had been caught sweetly reclining in the shadowy folds of some fleecy cloud, kissing the wife of the god of gods. These devils generally sympathized with man. There is in regard to them a most wonderful fact: In nearly all the theologies, mythologies and religions, the devils have been much more humane and merciful than the gods. No devil ever gave one of his generals an order to kill children and to rip open the bodies of pregnant women. Such barbarities were always ordered by the good gods. The pestilences were sent by the most merciful gods. The frightful famine, during which the dying child with pallid lips sucked the withered bosom of a dead mother, was sent by the loving gods. No devil was ever charged with such fiendish brutality.

One of these gods, according to the account, drowned an entire world, with the exception of eight persons. The old, the young, the beautiful and the helpless were remorsely devoured by the shoreless sea. This, the most fearful tragedy that the imagination of ignorant priests ever conceived, was the act, not of a devil, but of a god, so-called, whom men ignorantly worship unto this day. What a stain such an act would leave upon the character of a devil! One of the prophets of one of these gods, having in his power a captured king, hewed him in pieces in the sight of all the people. Was ever any imp of any devil guilty of such savagery?

One of these gods is reported to have given the following directions concerning human slavery: "If thou buy a Hebrew servant, six years shall he serve, and in the seventh he shall go out free for nothing. If he came in by himself, he shall go out by himself; if he were married, then his wife shall go out with him. If his master have given him a wife, and she have borne him sons or daughters, the wife and her children shall be her master's, and he shall go out by himself. And if the servant shall plainly say, I love my master, my wife and my children; I will not go out free. Then his master shall bring him unto the judges; he shall also bring him unto the door, or unto the door-post; and his master shall bore his ear through with an awl; and he shall serve him forever."

According to this, a man was given liberty upon condition that he would desert forever his wife and children. Did any devil ever force upon a husband, upon a father, so cruel and so heartless an alternative? Who can worship such a god? Who can bend the knee to such a monster? Who can pray to such a fiend?

All these gods threatened to torment forever the souls of their enemies. Did any devil ever make so infamous a threat? The basest thing recorded of the devil, is what he did concerning Job and his family, and that was done by the express permission of one of these gods, and to decide a little difference of opinion between their serene highnesses as to the character of " my servant Job."

The first account we have of the devil is found in that purely scientific book called Genesis, and is as follows: " Now the serpent was more subtile than any beast of the field which the Lord God had made, and he said unto the woman, Yea, hath God said, Ye shall not eat of the fruit of the trees of the garden? And the woman said unto the serpent, We may eat of the fruit of the trees of the garden; but of the fruit of the tree which is in the midst of the garden God hath said, Ye shall not eat of it, neither shall ye touch it, lest ye die. And the serpent said unto the woman, Ye shall not surely die. For God doth know that in the day ye eat thereof, then your eyes shall be opened and ye shall be as gods, knowing good and evil. And when the woman saw that the tree was good for food, and that it was pleasant to the eyes, and a tree to be desired to make one wise, she took of the fruit thereof and did eat, and gave also unto her husband with her, and he did eat. * *
And the Lord God said, Behold the man is be-

come as one of us, to know good and evil; and now, lest he put forth his hand, and take also of the tree of life and eat, and live forever. Therefore the Lord God sent him forth from the Garden of Eden to till the ground from which he was taken. So he drove out the man, and he placed at the east of the Garden of Eden cherubim and a flaming sword, which turned every way to keep the way of the tree of life."

According to this account the promise of the devil was fulfilled to the very letter. Adam and Eve did not die, and they did become as gods, knowing good and evil.

The account shows, however, that the gods dreaded education and knowledge then just as they do now. The church still faithfully guards the dangerous tree of knowledge, and has exerted in all ages her utmost power to keep mankind from eating the fruit thereof. The priests have never ceased repeating the old falsehood and the old threat: "Ye shall not eat of it, neither shall ye touch it, lest ye die." From every pulpit comes the same cry, born of the same fear: "Lest they eat and become as gods, knowing good and evil." For this reason, religion hates science, faith detests reason, theology is the sworn enemy of philosophy, and the church with its flaming sword still guards the hated tree, and like its supposed founder, curses to the lowest depths the brave thinkers who eat and become as gods.

If the account given in Genesis is really true, ought we not, after all, to thank this serpent? He was the first schoolmaster, the first advocate of learning, the first enemy of ignorance, the first to whisper in human ears the sacred word liberty, the creator of ambition, the author of modesty, of inquiry, of doubt, of investigation, of progress and of civilization.

Give me the storm and tempest of thought and action, rather than the dead calm of ignorance and faith! Banish me from Eden when you will; but first let me eat of the fruit of the tree of knowledge!

Some nations have borrowed their gods; of this number, we are compelled to say, is our own. The Jews having ceased to exist as a nation, and having no further use for a god, our ancestors appropriated him and adopted their devil at the same time. This borrowed god is still an object of some adoration, and this adopted devil still excites the apprehensions of our people. He is still supposed to be setting his traps and snares for the purpose of catching our unwary souls, and is still, with reasonable success, waging the old war against our God.

To me, it seems easy to account for these ideas concerning gods and devils. They are a perfectly natural production. Man has created them all, and under the same circumstances would create them again. Man has not only created all these gods, but he has created them out of the materials by which he has been surrounded. Generally he has modeled them after himself, and has given them hands, heads, feet, eyes, ears, and organs of speech. Each nation made its gods and devils speak its language not only, but put in their mouths the same mistakes in history, geography, astronomy, and in all matters of fact, generally made by the people. No god was ever in advance of the nation that created him. The negroes represented their deities with black skins and curly hair. The Mongolian gave to his a yellow complexion and dark almond-shaped eyes. The Jews were not allowed to paint theirs, or we should have seen Jehovah with a full beard, an oval face, and an aquiline nose. Zeus was a perfect Greek, and Jove looked as though a member of the Roman senate. The gods of Egypt had the patient face and placid look of the loving people who made them. The gods of northern countries were represented warmly clad in robes of fur; those of the tropics were naked. The gods of India were often mounted upon elephants; those of some islanders were great swimmers, and the deities of the Arctic zone were passionately fond of whale's blubber. Nearly all people have carved or painted representations of their gods, and these representations were, by the lower classes, generally treated as the real gods, and to these images and idols they addressed prayers and offered sacrifice.

"In some countries, even at this day, if the people after long praying do not obtain their desires, they turn their images off as impotent gods, or upbraid them in a most reproachful manner, loading them with blows and curses. 'How now, dog of a spirit,' they say, 'we give you lodging in a magnificent temple, we gild you with gold, feed you with the choicest food, and offer incense to you; yet, after all this care, you are so ungrateful as to refuse us what we ask.'

THE GODS. 25

Hereupon they will pull the god down and drag him through the filth of the street. If, in the meantime, it happens that they obtain their request, then, with a great deal of ceremony, they wash him clean, carry him back and place him in his temple again, where they fall down and make excuses for what they have done. 'Of a truth,' they say, 'we were a little too hasty, and you were a little too long in your grant. Why should you bring this beating on yourself. But what is done cannot be undone. Let us not think of it any more. If you will forget what is past we will gild you over brighter again than before.'"

Man has never been at a loss for gods. He has worshiped almost everything, including the vilest and most disgusting beasts. He has worshiped fire, earth, air, water, light, stars, and for hundreds of ages prostrated himself before enormous snakes. Savage tribes often make gods of articles they get from civilized people. The Todas worship a cow-bell. The Kotas worship two silver plates, which they regard as husband and wife, and another tribe manufactured a god out of a king of hearts.

Man, having always been the physical superior

of woman, accounts for the fact that most of the high gods have been males. Had woman been the physical superior, the powers supposed to be the rulers of Nature would have been women, and instead of being represented in the apparel of man, they would have luxuriated in trains, low-necked dresses, laces and back-hair.

Nothing can be plainer than that each nation gives to its god its peculiar characteristics, and that every individual gives to his god his personal peculiarities.

Man has no ideas, and can have none, except those suggested by his surroundings. He cannot conceive of anything utterly unlike what he has seen or felt. He can exaggerate, diminish, combine, separate, deform, beautify, improve, multiply and compare what he sees, what he feels, what he hears, and all of which he takes cognizance through the medium of the senses; but he cannot create. Having seen exhibitions of power, he can say, omnipotent. Having lived, he can say, immortality. Knowing something of time, he can say, eternity. Conceiving something of intelligence, he can say, God. Having seen exhibitions of malice, he can say, devil. A few gleams of happiness having fallen athwart the gloom of his life, he can say, heaven. Pain, in its numberless forms, having been experienced, he can say, hell. Yet all these ideas have a foundation in fact, and only a foundation. The superstructure has been reared by exaggerating, diminishing, combining, separating, deforming, beautifying, improving or multiplying realities, so that the edifice or fabric is but the incongruous grouping of what man has perceived through the medium of the senses. It is as though we should give to a lion the wings of an eagle, the hoofs of a bison, the tail of a horse, the pouch of a kangaroo, and the trunk of an elephant. We have in imagination created an impossible monster. And yet the various parts of this monster really exist. So it is with all the gods that man has made.

Beyond nature man cannot go even in thought —above nature he cannot rise—below nature he cannot fall.

Man, in his ignorance, supposed that all phenomena were produced by some intelligent powers, and with direct reference to him. To preserve friendly relations with these powers was, and still is, the object of all religions. Man knelt through fear and to implore assistance, or through gratitude for some favor which he supposed had been rendered. He endeavored by supplication to appease some being who, for some reason, had, as he believed, become enraged. The lightning and thunder terrified him. In the presence of the volcano he sank upon his knees. The great forests filled with wild and ferocious beasts, the monstrous serpents crawling in mysterious depths, the boundless sea, the flaming comets, the sinister eclipses, the awful calmness of the stars, and, more than all, the perpetual presence of death, convinced him that he was the sport and prey of unseen and malignant powers. The strange and frightful diseases to which he was subject, the freezings and burnings of fever, the contortions of epilepsy, the sudden palsies, the darkness of night, and the wild, terrible and fantastic dreams that filled his brain, satisfied him that he was haunted and pursued by countless spirits of evil. For some reason he supposed that these spirits differed in power— that they were not all alike malevolent—that the higher controlled the lower, and that his very existence depended upon gaining the assistance of the more powerful. For this purpose he resorted to prayer, to flattery, to worship and to sacrifice.

THE GODS.

These ideas appear to have been almost universal in savage man.

For ages all nations supposed that the sick and insane were possessed by evil spirits. For thousands of years the practice of medicine consisted in frightening these spirits away. Usually the priests would make the loudest and most discordant noises possible. They would blow horns, beat upon rude drums, clash cymbals, and in the meantime utter the most unearthly yells. If the noise-remedy failed, they would implore the aid of some more powerful spirit.

To pacify these spirits was considered of infinite importance. The poor barbarian, knowing that men could be softened by gifts, gave to these spirits that which to him seemed of the most value. With bursting heart he would offer the blood of his dearest child. It was impossible for him to conceive of a god utterly unlike himself, and he naturally supposed that these powers of the air would be affected a little at the sight of so great and so deep a sorrow. It was with the barbarian then as with the civilized now — one class lived upon and made merchandise of the fears of another. Certain persons took it upon themselves to appease the gods, and to instruct the people in their duties to these unseen powers. This was the origin of the priesthood. The priest pretended to stand between the wrath of the gods and the helplessness of man. He was man's attorney at the court of heaven. He carried to the invisible world a flag of truce, a protest and a request. He came back with a command, with authority and with power. Man fell upon his knees before his own servant, and the priest, taking advantage of the awe inspired by his supposed influence with the gods, made of his fellow-man a cringing hypocrite and slave. Even Christ, the supposed son of God, taught that persons were possessed of evil spirits, and frequently, according to the account, gave proof of his divine origin and mission by frightening droves of devils out of his unfortunate countrymen. Casting out devils was his principal employment, and the devils thus banished generally took occasion to acknowledge him as the true Messiah; which was not only very kind of them, but quite fortunate for him. The religious people have always regarded the testimony of these devils as perfectly conclusive, and the writers of the New Testament quote the words of these imps of darkness with great satisfaction.

The fact that Christ could withstand the temptations of the devil was considered as conclusive evidence that he was assisted by some god, or at least by some being superior to man. St. Matthew gives an account of an attempt made by the devil to tempt the supposed son of God; and it has always excited the wonder of Christians that the temptation was so nobly and heroically withstood. The account to which I refer is as follows:

"Then was Jesus led up of the spirit into the wilderness to be tempted of the devil. And when the tempter came to him, he said: 'If thou be the son of God, command that these stones be made bread.' But he answered, and said: 'It is written: man shall not live by bread alone, but by every word that proceedeth out of the mouth of God.' Then the devil taketh him up into the holy city and setteth him upon a pinnacle of the temple and saith unto him: 'If thou be the son of God, cast thyself down; for it is written, He shall give his angels charge concerning thee, lest at any time thou shalt dash thy foot against a stone.' Jesus said unto him: 'It is written again, thou shalt not tempt the Lord thy God.' Again the devil taketh him up into an exceeding high mountain and sheweth him all the kingdoms of the world and the glory of them, and saith unto him: 'All these will I give thee if thou wilt fall down and worship me.'"

The Christians now claim that Jesus was God. If he was God, of course the devil knew that fact, and yet, according to this account, the devil took the omnipotent God and placed him upon a pinnacle of the temple, and endeavored to induce him to dash himself against the earth. Failing in that, he took the creator, owner and governor of the universe up into an exceeding high mountain, and offered him this world — this grain of sand — if he, the God of all the worlds, would fall down and worship him, a poor devil, without even a tax title to one foot of dirt! Is it possible the devil was such an idiot? Should any great credit be given to this deity for not being caught with such chaff? Think of it! The devil — the prince of sharpers — the king of cunning — the master of finesse, trying to bribe God with a grain of sand that belonged to God!

Is there in all the religious literature of the world anything more grossly absurd than this?

These devils, according to the Bible, were of various kinds — some could speak and hear, others were deaf and dumb. All could not be cast out in the same way. The deaf and dumb spirits were quite difficult to deal with. St. Mark tells of a gentleman who brought his son to Christ. The boy, it seems, was possessed of a dumb spirit, over which the disciples had no control. "Jesus said unto the spirit: 'Thou dumb and deaf spirit, I charge thee come out of him, and enter no more into him.'" Whereupon, the deaf spirit (having heard what was said) cried out (being dumb) and immediately vacated the premises. The ease with which Christ controlled this deaf and dumb spirit excited the wonder of his disciples, and they asked him privately why they could not cast that spirit out. To whom he replied: "This kind can come forth by nothing but prayer and fasting." Is there a Christian in the whole world who would believe such a story if found in any other book? The trouble is, these pious people shut up their reason, and then open their Bible.

In the olden times the existence of devils was universally admitted. The people had no doubt upon that subject, and from such belief it followed as a matter of course, that a person, in order to vanquish these devils, had either to be a god, or to be assisted by one. All founders of religions have established their claims to divine origin by controlling evil spirits and suspending the laws of nature. Casting out devils was a certificate of divinity. A prophet, unable to cope with the powers of darkness was regarded with contempt. The utterance of the highest and noblest sentiments, the most blameless and holy life, commanded but little respect, unless accompanied by power to work miracles and command spirits.

This belief in good and evil powers had its origin in the fact that man was surrounded by what he was pleased to call good and evil phenomena. Phenomena affecting man pleasantly were ascribed to good spirits, while those affecting him unpleasantly or injuriously, were ascribed to evil spirits. It being admitted that all phenomena were produced by spirits, the spirits were divided according to the phenomena, and the phenomena were good or bad as they affected man.

Good spirits were supposed to be the authors of good phenomena, and evil spirits of the evil—so that the idea of a devil has been as universal as the idea of a god.

Many writers maintain that an idea to become universal must be true; that all universal ideas are innate, and that innate ideas cannot be false. If the fact that an idea has been universal proves that it is innate, and if the fact that an idea is innate proves that it is correct, then the believers in innate ideas must admit that the evidence of a god superior to nature, and of a devil superior to nature, is exactly the same, and that the existence of such a devil must be as self-evident as the existence of such a god. The truth is, a god was inferred from good, and a devil from bad, phenomena. And it is just as natural and logical to suppose that a devil would cause happiness as to suppose that a god would produce misery. Consequently, if an intelligence, infinite and supreme, is the immediate author of all phenomena, it is difficult to determine whether such intelligence is the friend or enemy of man. If phenomena were all good, we might say they were all produced by a perfectly beneficent being. If they were all bad, we might say they were produced by a perfectly malevolent power; but, as phenomena are, as they affect man, both good and bad, they must be produced by different and antagonistic spirits; by one who is sometimes actuated by kindness, and sometimes by malice; or all must be produced of necessity, and without reference to their consequences upon man.

The foolish doctrine that all phenomena can be traced to the interference of good and evil spirits, has been, and still is, almost universal. That most people still believe in some spirit that can change the natural order of events, is proven by the fact that nearly all resort to prayer. Thousands, at this very moment, are probably imploring some supposed power to interfere in their behalf. Some want health restored; some ask that the loved and absent be watched over and protected, some pray for riches, some for rain, some want diseases stayed, some vainly ask for food, some ask for revivals, a few ask for more wisdom, and now and then one tells the Lord to do as he may think best. Thousands ask to be protected from the devil; some, like David, pray for revenge, and some implore even God, not to lead

THE GODS.

them into temptation. All these prayers rest upon, and are produced by, the idea that some power not only can, but probably will, change the order of the universe. This belief has been among the great majority of tribes and nations. All sacred books are filled with the accounts of such interferences, and our own Bible is no exception to this rule.

If we believe in a power superior to nature, it is perfectly natural to suppose that such power can and will interfere in the affairs of this world. If there is no interference, of what practical use can such power be? The Scriptures give us the most wonderful accounts of divine interference: Animals talk like men; springs gurgle from dry bones; the sun and moon stop in the heavens in order that General Joshua may have more time to murder; the shadow on a dial goes back ten degrees to convince a petty king of a barbarous people that he is not going to die of a boil; fire refuses to burn; water positively declines to seek its level, but stands up like a wall; grains of sand become lice; common walking-sticks, to gratify a mere freak, twist themselves into serpents, and then swallow each other by way of exercise;

murmuring streams, laughing at the attraction of gravitation, run up hill for years, following wandering tribes from a pure love of frolic; prophecy becomes altogether easier than history; the sons of God become enamored of the world's girls; women are changed into salt for the purpose of keeping a great event fresh in the minds of men; an excellent article of brimstone is imported from heaven free of duty; clothes refuse to wear out for forty years; birds keep restaurants and feed wandering prophets free of expense; bears tear children in pieces for laughing at old men without wigs; muscular development depends upon the length of one's hair; dead people come to life, simply to get a joke on their enemies and heirs; witches and wizards converse freely with the souls of the departed, and God himself becomes a stone-cutter and engraver, after having been a tailor and dressmaker.

The veil between heaven and earth was always rent or lifted. The shadows of this world, the radiance of heaven, and the glare of hell mixed and mingled until man became uncertain as to which country he really inhabited. Man dwelt in an unreal world. He mistook his ideas,

THE GODS.

his dreams, for real things. His fears became terrible and malicious monsters. He lived in the midst of furies and fairies, nymphs and naiads, goblins and ghosts, witches and wizards, sprites and spooks, deities and devils. The obscure and gloomy depths were filled with claw and wing — with beak and hoof — with leering looks and sneering mouths — with the malice of deformity — with the cunning of hatred, and with all the slimy forms that fear can draw and paint upon the shadowy canvas of the dark.

It is enough to make one almost insane with pity to think what man in the long night has suffered; of the tortures he has endured, surrounded, as he supposed, by malignant powers and clutched by the fierce phantoms of the air. No wonder that he fell upon his trembling knees — that he built altars and reddened them even with his own blood. No wonder that he implored ignorant priests and impudent magicians for aid. No wonder that he crawled groveling in the dust to the temple's door, and there, in the insanity of despair, besought the deaf gods to hear his bitter cry of agony and fear.

The savage as he emerges from a state of bar-

barism, gradually loses faith in his idols of wood and stone, and in their place puts a multitude of spirits. As he advances in knowledge, he generally discards the petty spirits, and in their stead believes in one, whom he supposes to be infinite and supreme. Supposing this great spirit to be superior to nature, he offers worship or flattery in exchange for assistance. At last, finding that he obtains no aid from this supposed deity — finding that every search after the absolute must of necessity end in failure — finding that man cannot by any possibility conceive of the conditionless — he begins to investigate the facts by which he is surrounded, and to depend upon himself.

The people are beginning to think, to reason and to investigate. Slowly, painfully, but surely, the gods are being driven from the earth. Only upon rare occasions are they, even by the most religious, supposed to interfere in the affairs of men. In most matters we are at last supposed to be free. Since the invention of steamships and railways, so that the products of all countries can be easily interchanged, the gods have quit the business of producing famine. Now and then they kill a child because it is idolized by its parents. As a rule they have given up causing accidents on railroads, exploding boilers, and bursting kerosene lamps. Cholera, yellow fever, and small-pox are still considered heavenly weapons; but measles, itch and ague are now attributed to natural causes. As a general thing, the gods have stopped drowning children, except as a punishment for violating the Sabbath. They still pay some attention to the affairs of kings, men of genius and persons of great wealth; but ordinary people are left to shirk for themselves as best they may. In wars between great nations, the gods still interfere; but in prize fights, the best man with an honest referee, is almost sure to win.

The church cannot abandon the idea of special providence. To give up that doctrine is to give up all. The church must insist that prayer is answered — that some power superior to nature hears and grants the request of the sincere and humble Christian, and that this same power in some mysterious way provides for all.

A devout clergyman sought every opportunity to impress upon the mind of his son the fact, that God takes care of all his creatures; that the falling sparrow attracts his attention, and that his loving kindness is over all his works. Happening, one day, to see a crane wading in quest of food, the good man pointed out to his son the perfect adaptation of the crane to get his living in that manner. "See," said he, "how his legs are formed for wading! What a long slender bill he has! Observe how nicely he folds his feet when putting them in or drawing them out of the water! He does not cause the slightest ripple. He is thus enabled to approach the fish without giving them any notice of his arrival." "My son," said he, "it is impossible to look at that bird without recognizing the design, as well as the goodness of God, in thus providing the means of subsistence." "Yes," replied the boy, "I think I see the goodness of God, at least so far as the crane is concerned; but after all, father, don't you think the arrangement a little tough on the fish?"

Even the advanced religionist, although disbelieving in any great amount of interference by the gods in this age of the world, still thinks, that in the beginning, some god made the laws governing the universe. He believes that in consequence of these laws a man can lift a greater weight with, than without, a lever; that this god so made matter, and so established the order of things, that two bodies cannot occupy the same space at the same time; so that a body once put in motion will keep moving until it is stopped; so that it is a greater distance around, than across a circle; so that a perfect square has four equal sides, instead of five or seven. He insists that it took a direct interposition of Providence to make the whole greater than a part, and that had it not been for this power superior to nature, twice one might have been more than twice two, and sticks and strings might have had only one end apiece. Like the old Scotch divine, he thanks God that Sunday comes at the end instead of in the middle of the week, and that death comes at the close instead of at the commencement of life, thereby giving us time to prepare for that holy day and that most solemn event. These religious people see nothing but design everywhere, and personal, intelligent interference in everything. They insist that the universe has been created, and that the adaptation of means to ends is perfectly apparent. They point us to the sunshine, to the flowers, to the April rain, and to all there is of beauty and of use in the world. Did it ever occur to them that a cancer is as beautiful in its development as is the reddest rose? That what they are pleased to call the adaptation of means to ends, is as apparent in the cancer as in the April rain? How beautiful the process of digestion! By what ingenious methods the blood is poisoned so that the cancer shall have food! By what wonderful contrivances the entire system of man is made to pay tribute to this divine and charming cancer! See by what admirable instrumentalities it feeds itself from the surrounding quivering, dainty flesh! See how it gradually but surely expands and grows! By what marvelous mechanism it is supplied with long and slender roots that reach out to the most secret nerves of pain for sustenance and life! What beautiful colors it presents! Seen through the microscope it is a miracle of order and beauty. All the ingenuity of man cannot stop its growth. Think of the amount of thought it must have required to invent a way by which the life of one man might be given to produce one cancer? Is it possible to look upon it and doubt that there is design in the universe, and that the inventor of this wonderful cancer must be infinitely powerful, ingenious and good?

We are told that the universe was designed and created, and that it is absurd to suppose that matter has existed from eternity; but that it is perfectly self-evident that a god has.

If a god created the universe, then, there must have been a time when he commenced to create. Back of that time there must have been an eternity, during which there had existed nothing— absolutely nothing — except this supposed god. According to this theory, this god spent an eternity, so to speak, in an infinite vacuum, and in perfect idleness.

Admitting that a god did create the universe, the question then arises, of what did he create it? It certainly was not made of nothing. Nothing, considered in the light of a raw material, is a most decided failure. It follows, then, that the god must have made the universe out of himself, he being the only existence. The universe is material, and if it was made of god, the god must have been material. With this very thought in his mind, Anaximander of Miletus said: "Creation is the decomposition of the infinite."

It has been demonstrated that the earth would fall to the sun, only for the fact, that it is attracted by other worlds, and those worlds must be attracted by other worlds still beyond them, and so on, without end. This proves the material universe to be infinite. If an infinite universe has been made out of an infinite god, how much of the god is left?

The idea of a creative deity is gradually being abandoned, and nearly all truly scientific minds admit that matter must have existed from eternity. It is indestructible, and the indestructible cannot be created. It is the crowning glory of our century to have demonstrated the indestructibility and the eternal persistence of force. Neither matter nor force can be increased nor diminished. Force cannot exist apart from matter. Matter exists only in connection with force, and consequently, a force apart from matter, and superior to nature, is a demonstrated impossibility.

Force, then, must have also existed from eternity, and could not have been created. Matter in its countless forms, from dead earth to the eyes of those we love, and force, in all its manifestations, from simple motion to the grandest thought, deny creation and defy control.

Thought is a form of force. We walk with the same force with which we think. Man is an organism, that changes several forms of force into thought-force. Man is a machine into which we put what we call food, and produce what we call thought. Think of that wonderful chemistry by which bread was changed into the divine tragedy of Hamlet!

A god must not only be material, but he must be an organism, capable of changing other forms of force into thought-force. This is what we call eating. Therefore, if the god thinks, he must eat, that is to say, he must of necessity have some means of supplying the force with which to think. It is impossible to conceive of a being who can eternally impart force to matter, and yet have no means of supplying the force thus imparted.

If neither matter nor force were created, what evidence have we, then, of the existence of a power superior to nature? The theologian will probably reply, "We have law and order, cause and effect, and beside all this, matter could not have put itself in motion."

Suppose, for the sake of the argument, that there is no being superior to nature, and that matter and force have existed from eternity. Now, suppose that two atoms should come together, would there be an effect? Yes. Suppose they came in exactly opposite directions with equal force, they would be stopped, to say the least. This would be an effect. If this is so, then you have matter, force and effect without a being superior to nature. Now, suppose that two other atoms, just like the first two, should come together under precisely the same circumstances, would not the effect be exactly the same? Yes. Like causes, producing like effects, is what we mean by law and order. Then we have matter, force, effect, law and order without a being superior to nature. Now, we know that every effect must also be a cause, and that every cause must be an effect. The atoms coming together did produce an effect, and as every effect must also be a cause, the effect produced by the collision of the atoms, must as to something else have been a cause. Then we have matter, force, law, order, cause and effect without a being superior to nature. Nothing is left for the supernatural but empty space. His throne is a void, and his boasted realm is without matter, without force, without law, without cause, and without effect.

But what put all this matter in motion? If matter and force have existed from eternity, then matter must have always been in motion. There can be no force without motion. Force is forever active, and there is, and there can be no cessation. If, therefore, matter and force have existed from eternity, so has motion. In the whole universe there is not even one atom in a state of rest.

A deity outside of nature exists in nothing, and is nothing. Nature embraces with infinite arms all matter and all force. That which is beyond her grasp is destitute of both, and can hardly be worth the worship and adoration even of a man.

There is but one way to demonstrate the existence of a power independent of and superior to nature, and that is by breaking, if only for one moment, the continuity of cause and effect. Pluck from the endless chain of existence one little link; stop for one instant the grand procession, and you have shown beyond all contradiction that nature has a master. Change the fact, just for one second, that matter attracts matter, and a god appears.

The rudest savage has always known this fact, and for that reason always demanded the evidence of miracle. The founder of a religion must be able to turn water into wine — cure with a word the blind and lame, and raise with a simple touch the dead to life. It was necessary for him to demonstrate to the satisfaction of his barbarian disciple, that he was superior to nature. In times of ignorance this was easy to do. The credulity of the savage was almost boundless. To him the marvelous was the beautiful, the mysterious was the sublime. Consequently, every religion has for its foundation a miracle — that is to say, a violation of nature — that is to say, a falsehood.

No one, in the world's whole history, ever attempted to substantiate a truth by a miracle. Truth scorns the assistance of miracle. Nothing but falsehood ever attested itself by signs and wonders. No miracle ever was performed, and no sane man ever thought he had performed one, and until one is performed, there can be no evidence of the existence of any power superior to, and independent of nature.

The church wishes us to believe. Let the church, or one of its intellectual saints, perform a miracle, and we will believe. We are told that nature has a superior. Let this superior, for one single instant, control nature, and we will admit the truth of your assertions.

We have heard talk enough. We have listened to all the drowsy, idealess, vapid sermons that we wish to hear. We have read your Bible and the works of your best minds. We have heard your prayers, your solemn groans and your reverential amens. All these amount to less than nothing. We want one fact. We beg at the doors of your churches for just one little fact. We pass our hats along your pews and under your pulpits and implore you for just one fact. We know all about your mouldy wonders and your stale miracles. We want a this year's fact. We ask only one. Give us one fact for charity. Your miracles are too ancient. The witnesses have been dead for nearly two thousand years. Their reputation for "truth and veracity" in the neighborhood where they resided is wholly unknown to us. Give us a new miracle, and substantiate it by witnesses who still have the cheerful habit of living in this world. Do not send us to Jericho to hear the winding horns, nor put us in the fire with Shadrach, Meshech, and Abednego. Do not compel us to navigate the sea with Captain Jonah, nor dine with Mr. Ezekiel. There is no sort of use in sending us fox-hunting with Samson. We have positively lost all interest in that little speech so eloquently delivered by Balaam's inspired donkey. It is worse than useless to show us fishes with money in their mouths, and call our attention to vast multitudes stuffing themselves with five crackers and two sardines. We demand a new miracle, and we demand it now. Let the church furnish at least one, or forever after hold her peace.

In the olden time, the church, by violating the order of nature, proved the existence of her God. At that time miracles were performed with the most astonishing ease. They became so common that the church ordered her priests to desist. And now this same church — the people having found some little sense — admits, not only, that she cannot perform a miracle, but insists that the absence of miracle — the steady, unbroken march of cause and effect, proves the existence of a power superior to nature. The fact is, however, that the indissoluble chain of cause and effect proves exactly the contrary.

Sir William Hamilton, one of the pillars of modern theology, in discussing this very subject, uses the following language: "The phenomena of matter taken by themselves, so far from warranting any inference to the existence of a god, would on the contrary ground even an argument to his negation. The phenomena of the material world are subjected to immutable laws; are produced and reproduced in the same invariable succession, and manifest only the blind force of a mechanical necessity."

Nature is but an endless series of efficient causes. She cannot create, but she eternally transforms. There was no beginning, and there can be no end.

The best minds, even in the religious world, admit that in material nature there is no evidence of what they are pleased to call a god. They find their evidence in the phenomena of intelligence, and very innocently assert that intelligence is above, and in fact, opposed to nature. They insist that man, at least, is a special creation; that he has somewhere in his brain a divine spark, a little portion of the "Great First Cause." They say that matter cannot produce thought; but that thought can produce matter. They tell us that man has intelligence, and therefore there must be an intelligence greater than his. Why not say, God has intelligence, therefore there must be an intelligence greater than his? So far as we know, there is no intelligence apart from matter. We cannot conceive of thought, except as produced within a brain.

The science, by means of which they demonstrate the existence of an impossible intelligence, and an incomprehensible power is called, metaphysics or theology. The theologians admit that the phenomena of matter tend, at least, to disprove the existence of any power superior to

THE GODS.

nature, because in such phenomena we see nothing but an endless chain of efficient causes — nothing but the force of a mechanical necessity. They therefore appeal to what they denominate the phenomena of mind to establish this superior power.

The trouble is, that in the phenomena of mind we find the same endless chain of efficient causes; the same mechanical necessity. Every thought must have had an efficient cause. Every motive, every desire, every fear, hope and dream must have been necessarily produced. There is no room in the mind of man for providence or chance. The facts and forces governing thought are as absolute as those governing the motions of the planets. A poem is produced by the forces of nature, and is as necessarily and naturally produced as mountains and seas. You will seek in vain for a thought in man's brain without its efficient cause. Every mental operation is the necessary result of certain facts and conditions. Mental phenomena are considered more complicated than those of matter, and consequently more mysterious. Being more mysterious, they are considered better evidence of the existence of a god. No one infers a god from the simple, from the known, from what is understood, but from the complex, from the unknown, and incomprehensible. Our ignorance is God; what we know is science.

When we abandon the doctrine that some infinite being created matter and force, and enacted a code of laws for their government, the idea of interference will be lost. The real priest will then be, not the mouth-piece of some pretended deity, but the interpreter of nature. From that moment the church ceases to exist. The tapers will die out upon the dusty altar; the moths will eat the fading velvet of pulpit and pew; the Bible will take its place with the Shastras, Puranas, Vedas, Eddas, Sagas and Korans, and the fetters of a degrading faith will fall from the minds of men.

"But," says the religionist, "you cannot explain everything; you cannot understand everything; and that which you cannot explain, that which you do not comprehend, is my God."

We are explaining more every day. We are understanding more every day; consequently your God is growing smaller every day.

THE GODS.

Nothing daunted, the religionist then insists that nothing can exist without a cause, except cause, and that this uncaused cause is God.

To this we again reply: Every cause must produce an effect, because until it does produce an effect, it is not a cause. Every effect must in its turn become a cause. Therefore, in the nature of things, there cannot be a last cause, for the reason that a so-called last cause would necessarily produce an effect, and that effect must of necessity becomes a cause. The converse of these propositions must be true. Every effect must have had a cause, and every cause must have been an effect. Therefore there could have been no first cause. A first cause is just as impossible as a last effect.

Beyond the universe there is nothing, and within the universe the supernatural does not and cannot exist.

The moment these great truths are understood and admitted, a belief in general or special providence become impossible. From that instant men will cease their vain efforts to please an imaginary being, and will give their time and attention to the affairs of this world. They will abandon the idea of attaining any object by prayer and supplication. The element of uncertainty will, in a great measure, be removed from the domain of the future, and man, gathering courage from a succession of victories over the obstructions of nature, will attain a serene grandeur unknown to the disciples of any superstition. The plans of mankind will no longer be interfered with by the finger of a supposed omnipotence, and no one will believe that nations or individuals are protected or destroyed by any deity whatever. Science, freed from the chains of pious custom and evangelical prejudice, will, within her sphere, be supreme. The mind will investigate without reverence, and publish its conclusions without fear. Agassiz will no longer hesitate to declare the Mosaic cosmogony utterly inconsistent with the demonstrated truths of geology, and will cease pretending any reverence for the Jewish Scriptures. The moment science succeeds in rendering the church powerless for evil, the real thinkers will be outspoken. The little flags of truce carried by timid philosophers will disappear, and the cowardly parley will give place to victory — lasting and universal.

If we admit that some infinite being has controlled the destinies of persons and peoples, history becomes a most cruel and bloody farce. Age after age, the strong have trampled upon the weak; the crafty and heartless have ensnared and enslaved the simple and innocent, and nowhere, in all the annals of mankind, has any god succored the oppressed.

Man should cease to expect aid from on high. By this time he should know that heaven has no ear to hear, and no hand to help. The present is the necessary child of all the past. There has been no chance, and there can be no interference.

If abuses are destroyed, man must destroy them. If slaves are freed, man must free them. If new truths are discovered, man must discover them. If the naked are clothed; if the hungry are fed; if justice is done; if labor is rewarded; if superstition is driven from the mind; if the defenceless are protected and if the right finally triumphs, all must be the work of man. The grand victories of the future must be won by man, and by man alone.

Nature, so far as we can discern, without passion and without intention, forms, transforms, and retransforms forever. She neither weeps nor rejoices. She produces man without purpose, and obliterates him without regret. She knows no distinction between the beneficial and the hurtful. Poison and nutrition, pain and joy, life and death, smiles and tears are alike to her. She is neither merciful nor cruel. She cannot be flattered by worship nor melted by tears. She does not know even the attitude of prayer. She appreciates no difference between poison in the fangs of snakes and mercy in the hearts of men. Only through man does nature take cognizance of the good, the true, and the beautiful; and, so far as we know, man is the highest intelligence.

And yet man continues to believe that there is some power independent of and superior to nature, and still endeavors, by form, ceremony, supplication, hypocrisy and sacrifice, to obtain its aid. His best energies have been wasted in the service of this phantom. The horrors of witchcraft were all born of an ignorant belief in the existence of a totally depraved being superior to nature, acting in perfect independence of her laws; and all religious superstition has had for its basis a belief in at least two beings, one good and the other bad, both of whom could arbitrarily change the order of the universe. The history of religion is simply the story of man's efforts in all ages to avoid one of these powers, and to pacify the other. Both powers have inspired little else than abject fear. The cold, calculating sneer of the devil, and the frown of God, were equally terrible. In any event, man's fate was to be arbitrarily fixed forever by an unknown power superior to all law, and to all fact. Until this belief is thrown aside, man must consider himself the slave of phantom masters — neither of whom promise liberty in this world nor in the next.

Man must learn to rely upon himself. Reading bibles will not protect him from the blasts of winter, but houses, fires, and clothing will. To prevent famine, one plow is worth a million sermons, and even patent medicines will cure more diseases than all the prayers uttered since the beginning of the world.

Although many eminent men have endeavored to harmonize necessity and free will, the existence of evil, and the infinite power and good ness of God, they have succeeded only in producing learned and ingenious failures. Immense efforts have been made to reconcile ideas utterly inconsistent with the facts by which we are surrounded, and all persons who have failed to perceive the pretended reconciliation, have been denounced as infidels, atheists and scoffers. The whole power of the church has been brought to bear against philosophers and scientists in order to compel a denial of the authority of demonstration, and to induce some Judas to betray Reason, one of the saviors of mankind.

During that frightful period known as the "Dark Ages," Faith reigned, with scarcely a rebellious subject. Her temples were "carpeted with knees," and the wealth of nations adorned her countless shrines. The great painters prostituted their genius to immortalize her vagaries, while the poets enshrined them in song. At her bidding, man covered the earth with blood. The scales of Justice were turned with her gold, and for her use were invented all the cunning instruments of pain. She built cathedrals for God, and dungeons for men. She peopled the clouds with angels and the earth with slaves. For centuries the world was retracing its steps—going steadily back toward barbaric night! A few infidels — a few heretics cried, "Halt!" to the great rabble of ignorant devotion, and made it possible for the genius of the nineteenth century to revolutionize the cruel creeds and superstitions of mankind.

The thoughts of man, in order to be of any real worth, must be free. Under the influence of fear the brain is paralyzed, and instead of bravely solving a problem for itself, tremblingly adopts the solution of another. As long as a majority of men will cringe to the very earth before some petty prince or king, what must be the infinite abjectness of their little souls in the presence of their supposed creator and God? Under such circumstances, what can their thoughts be worth?

The originality of repetition, and the mental vigor of acquiescence, are all that we have any right to expect from the Christian world. As long as every question is answered by the word "God," scientific inquiry is simply impossible. As fast as phenomena are satisfactorily explained the domain of the power, supposed to be superior to nature must decrease, while the horizon of the known must as constantly continue to enlarge.

It is no longer satisfactory to account for the fall and rise of nations by saying, "It is the will of God." Such an explanation puts ignorance and education upon an exact equality, and does away with the idea of really accounting for anything whatever.

Will the religionist pretend that the real end of science is to ascertain how and why God acts? Science, from such a standpoint would consist in investigating the law of arbitrary action, and in a grand endeavor to ascertain the rules necessarily obeyed by infinite caprice.

From a philosophical point of view, science is knowledge of the laws of life; of the conditions of happiness; of the facts by which we are surrounded, and the relations we sustain to men and things — by means of which, man, so to speak, subjugates nature and bends the elemental powers to his will, making blind force the servant of his brain.

A belief in special providence does away with the spirit of investigation, and is inconsistent with personal effort. Why should man endeavor to thwart the designs of God? Which of you, by taking thought, can add one cubit to his stature? Under the influence of this belief, man, basking in the sunshine of a delusion, considers the lilies of the field and refuses to take any thought for the morrow. Believing himself in the power of an infinite being, who can, at any moment, dash him to the lowest hell or raise him to the highest heaven, he necessarily abandons the idea of accomplishing anything by his own efforts. As long as this belief was general, the world was filled with ignorance, superstition and misery. The energies of man were wasted in a vain effort to obtain the aid of this power, supposed to be superior to nature. For countless ages, even men were sacrificed upon the altar of this impossible god. To please him, mothers have shed the blood of their own babes; martyrs have chanted triumphant songs in the midst of flame; priests have gorged themselves with blood; nuns have forsworn the ecstasies of love; old men have tremblingly implored; women have sobbed and entreated; every pain has been endured, and every horror has been perpetrated.

Through the dim long years that have fled,

humanity has suffered more than can be conceived. Most of the misery has been endured by the weak, the loving and the innocent. Women have been treated like poisonous beasts, and little children trampled upon as though they had been vermin. Numberless altars have been reddened, even with the blood of babes; beautiful girls have been given to slimy serpents; whole races of men doomed to centuries of slavery, and everywhere there has been outrage beyond the power of genius to express. During all these years the suffering have supplicated; the withered lips of famine have prayed; the pale victims have implored, and Heaven has been deaf and blind.

Of what use have the gods been to man?

It is no answer to say that some god created the world, established certain laws, and then turned his attention to other matters, leaving his children weak, ignorant and unaided, to fight the battle of life alone. It is no solution to declare that in some other world this god will render a few, or even all, his subjects happy. What right have we to expect that a perfectly wise, good and powerful being will ever do better than he has done, and is doing? The world is filled with imperfections. If it was made by an infinite being, what reason have we for saying that he will render it nearer perfect than it now is? If the infinite "Father" allows a majority of his children to live in ignorance and wretchedness now, what evidence is there that he will ever improve their condition? Will God have more power? Will he become more merciful? Will his love for his poor creatures increase? Can the conduct of infinite wisdom, power and love ever change? Is the infinite capable of any improvement whatever?

We are informed by the clergy that this world is a kind of school; that the evils by which we are surrounded are for the purpose of developing our souls, and that only by suffering can men become pure, strong, virtuous and grand.

Supposing this to be true, what is to become of those who die in infancy? The little children, according to this philosophy, can never be developed. They were so unfortunate as to escape the ennobling influences of pain and misery, and as a consequence, are doomed to an eternity of mental inferiority. If the clergy are right on this question, none are so unfortunate as the happy, and we should envy only the suffering and distressed. If evil is necessary to the development of man, in this life, how is it possible for the soul to improve in the perfect joy of Paradise?

Since Paley found his watch, the argument of "design" has been relied upon as unanswerable. The church teaches that this world, and all that it contains, were created substantially as we now see them; that the grasses, the flowers, the trees, and all animals, including man, were special creations, and that they sustain no necessary relation to each other. The most orthodox will admit that some earth has been washed into the sea; that the sea has encroached a little upon the land, and that some mountains may be a trifle lower than in the morning of creation. The theory of gradual development was unknown to our fathers; the idea of evolution did not occur to them. Our fathers looked upon the then arrangement of things as the primal arrangement. The earth appeared to them fresh from the hands of a deity. They knew nothing of the slow evolutions of countless years, but supposed that the almost infinite variety of vegetable and animal forms had existed from the first.

Suppose that upon some island we should find a man a million years of age, and suppose that we should find him in the possession of a most beautiful carriage, constructed upon the most perfect model. And suppose, further, that he should tell us that it was the result of several hundred thousand years of labor and of thought; that for fifty thousand years he used as flat a log as he could find, before it occurred to him, that by splitting the log, he could have the same surface with only half the weight; that it took him many thousand years to invent wheels for this log; that the wheels he first used were solid, and that fifty thousand years of thought suggested the use of spokes and tire; that for many centuries he used the wheels without linch-pins; that it took a hundred thousand years more to think of using four wheels, instead of two; that for ages he walked behind the carriage, when going down hill, in order to hold it back, and that only by a lucky chance he invented the tongue; would we conclude that this man, from the very first, had been an infinitely ingenious and perfect mechanic? Suppose we found him living in an elegant mansion, and he should inform us that he lived in that house for five hundred thousand years before he thought of putting on a roof, and that he had but recently invented windows and doors; would we say that from the beginning he had been an infinitely accomplished and scientific architect?

Does not an improvement in the things created, show a corresponding improvement in the creator?

Would an infinitely wise, good and powerful God, intending to produce man, commence with the lowest possible forms of life; with the simplest organism that can be imagined, and during immeasurable periods of time, slowly and almost imperceptibly improve upon the rude beginning, until man was evolved? Would countless ages thus be wasted in the production of awkward forms, afterwards abandoned? Can the intelligence of man discover the least wisdom in covering the earth with crawling, creeping horrors, that live only upon the agonies and pangs of others? Can we see the propriety of so constructing the earth, that only an insignificant portion of its surface is capable of producing an intelligent man? Who can appreciate the mercy of so making the world that all animals devour animals; so that every mouth is a slaughter-house, and every stomach a tomb? Is it possible to discover infinite intelligence and love in universal and eternal carnage?

What would we think of a father, who should give a farm to his children, and before giving them possession should plant upon it thousands of deadly shrubs and vines; should stock it with ferocious beasts, and poisonous reptiles; should take pains to put a few swamps in the neighborhood to breed malaria; should so arrange matters, that the ground would occasionally open and swallow a few of his darlings, and besides all this, should establish a few volcanoes in the immediate vicinity, that might at any moment overwhelm his children with rivers of fire? Suppose that this father neglected to tell his children which of the plants were deadly; that the reptiles were poisonous; failed to say anything about the earthquakes, and kept the volcano business a profound secret; would we pronounce him angel or fiend?

And yet this is exactly what the orthodox God has done.

According to the theologians, God prepared this globe expressly for the habitation of his loved children, and yet he filled the forests with ferocious beasts; placed serpents in every path; stuffed the world with earthquakes, and adorned its surface with mountains of flame.

Notwithstanding all this, we are told that the world is perfect; that it was created by a perfect being, and is therefore necessarily perfect. The next moment, these same persons will tell us that the world was cursed; covered with brambles, thistles and thorns, and that man was doomed to disease and death, simply because our poor, dear mother ate an apple contrary to the command of an arbitrary God.

A very pious friend of mine, having heard that I had said the world was full of imperfections, asked me if the report was true. Upon being informed that it was, he expressed great surprise that any one could be guilty of such presumption. He said that, in his judgment, it was impossible to point out an imperfection. "Be kind enough," said he, "to name even one improvement that you could make, if you had the power." "Well," said I, "I would make good health catching, instead of disease." The truth is, it is impossible to harmonize all the ills, and pains, and agonies of this world with the idea that we were created by, and are watched over and protected by an infinitely wise, powerful and beneficent God, who is superior to and independent of nature.

The clergy, however, balance all the real ills of this life with the expected joys of the next. We are assured that all is perfection in heaven — there the skies are cloudless — there all is serenity and peace. Here empires may be overthrown; dynasties may be extinguished in blood; millions of slaves may toil 'neath the fierce rays of the sun, and the cruel strokes of the lash; yet all is happiness in heaven. Pestilences may strew the earth with corpses of the loved; the survivors may bend above them in agony — yet the placid bosom of heaven is unruffled. Children may expire vainly asking for bread; babes may be devoured by serpents, while the gods sit smiling in the clouds. The innocent may languish unto death in the obscurity of dungeons;

brave men and heroic women may be changed to ashes at the bigot's stake, while heaven is filled with song and joy. Out on the wide sea, in darkness and in storm, the shipwrecked struggle with the cruel waves while the angels play upon their golden harps. The streets of the world are filled with the diseased, the deformed and the helpless; the chambers of pain are crowded with the pale forms of the suffering, while the angels float and fly in the happy realms of day. In heaven they are too happy to have sympathy; too busy singing to aid the imploring and distressed. Their eyes are blinded; their ears are stopped and their hearts are turned to stone by the infinite selfishness of joy. The saved mariner is too happy when he touches the shore to give a moment's thought to his drowning brothers. With the indifference of happiness, with the contempt of bliss, heaven barely glances at the miseries of earth. Cities are devoured by the rushing lava; the earth opens and thousands perish; women raise their clasped hands towards heaven, but the gods are too happy to aid their children. The smiles of the deities are unacquainted with the tears of men. The shouts of heaven drown the sobs of earth.

THE GODS.

Having shown how man created gods, and how he became the trembling slave of his own creation, the questions naturally arise: How did he free himself even a little, from these monarchs of the sky, from these despots of the clouds, from this aristocracy of the air? How did he, even to the extent that he has, outgrow his ignorant, abject terror, and throw off the yoke of superstition?

Probably, the first thing that tended to disabuse his mind was the discovery of order, of regularity, of periodicity in the universe. From this he began to suspect that everything did not happen purely with reference to him. He noticed, that whatever he might do, the motions of the planets were always the same; that eclipses were periodical, and that even comets came at certain intervals. This convinced him that eclipses and comets had nothing to do with him, and that his conduct had nothing to do with them. He perceived that they were not caused for his benefit or injury. He thus learned to regard them with admiration instead of fear. He began to suspect that famine was not sent by some enraged and revengeful deity, but resulted often from the neglect and ignorance of man. He learned that diseases were not produced by evil spirits. He found that sickness was occasioned by natural causes, and could be cured by natural means. He demonstrated, to his own satisfaction at least, that prayer is not a medicine. He found by sad experience that his gods were of no practical use, as they never assisted him, except when he was perfectly able to help himself. At last, he began to discover that his individual action had nothing whatever to do with strange appearances in the heavens; that it was impossible for him to be bad enough to cause a whirlwind, or good enough to stop one. After many centuries of thought, he about half concluded that making mouths at a priest would not necessarily cause an earthquake. He noticed, and no doubt with considerable astonishment, that very good men were occasionally struck by lightning, while very bad ones escaped. He was frequently forced to the painful conclusion (and it is the most painful to which any human being ever was forced) that the right did not always prevail. He noticed that the gods did not interfere in behalf of the weak and innocent. He was now and then astonished by seeing an unbeliever in the enjoyment of most excellent health. He finally ascertained that there could be no possible connection between an unusually severe winter and his failure to give a sheep to a priest. He began to suspect that the order of the universe was not constantly being changed to assist him because he repeated a creed. He observed that some children would steal after having been regularly baptized. He noticed a vast difference between religion and justice, and that the worshipers of the same god, took delight in cutting each other's throats. He saw that these religious disputes filled the world with hatred and slavery. At last he had the courage to suspect, that no god at any time interferes with the order of events. He learned a few facts, and these facts positively refused to harmonize with the ignorant superstitions of his fathers. Finding his sacred books incorrect and false in some particulars, his faith in their authenticity began to be shaken; finding his priests ignorant upon some points, he began to lose respect for the cloth. This was the commencement of intellectual freedom.

The civilization of man has increased just to the same extent that religious power has decreased. The intellectual advancement of man depends upon how often he can exchange an old superstition for a new truth. The church never enabled a human being to make even one of these exchanges; on the contrary, all her power has been used to prevent them. In spite, however, of the church, man found that some of his religious conceptions were wrong. By reading his Bible, he found that the ideas of his God were more cruel and brutal than those of the most depraved savage. He also discovered that this holy book was filled with ignorance, and that it must have been written by persons wholly unacquainted with the nature of the phenomena by which we are surrounded; and now and then, some man had the goodness and courage to speak his honest thoughts. In every age some thinker, some doubter, some investigator, some hater of hypocrisy, some despiser of sham, some brave lover of the right, has gladly, proudly and heroically braved the ignorant fury of superstition for the sake of man and truth. These divine men were generally torn in pieces by the worshipers of the gods. Socrates was poisoned because he lacked reverence for some of the deities. Christ was crucified by a religious rabble for the crime of blasphemy. Nothing is more gratifying to a religionist than to destroy his enemies at the command of God. Religious persecution springs from a due admixture of love towards God and hatred towards man.

The terrible religious wars that inundated the world with blood tended at least to bring all religion into disgrace and hatred. Thoughtful people began to question the divine origin of a religion that made its believers hold the rights of others in absolute contempt. A few began to compare Christianity with the religions of heathen people, and were forced to admit that the difference was hardly worth dying for. They also found that other nations were even happier and more prosperous than their own. They began to suspect that their religion, after all, was not of much real value.

For three hundred years the Christian world endeavored to rescue from the "Infidel" the empty sepulchre of Christ. For three hundred years the armies of the cross were baffled and beaten by the victorious hosts of an impudent impostor. This immense fact sowed the seeds of distrust throughout all Christendom, and millions began to lose confidence in a God who had been vanquished by Mohammed. The people also found that commerce made friends where religion made enemies, and that religious zeal was utterly incompatible with peace between nations or individuals. They discovered that those who loved the gods most were apt to love men least; that the arrogance of universal forgiveness was amazing; that the most malicious had the effrontery to pray for their enemies, and that humility and tyranny were the fruit of the same tree.

For ages, a deadly conflict has been waged between a few brave men and women of thought and genius upon the one side, and the great ignorant religious mass on the other. This is the war between Science and Faith. The few have appealed to reason, to honor, to law, to freedom, to the known, and to happiness here in this world. The many have appealed to prejudice, to fear, to miracle, to slavery, to the unknown, and to misery hereafter. The few have said, "Think!" The many have said, "Believe!"

The first doubt was the womb and cradle of progress, and from the first doubt, man has continued to advance. Men began to investigate, and the church began to oppose. The astronomer scanned the heavens, while the church branded his grand forehead with the word, "Infidel;" and now, not a glittering star in all the vast expanse bears a Christian name. In spite of all religion, the geologist penetrated the earth, read her history in books of stone, and found, hidden within her bosom, souvenirs of all the ages. Old ideas perished in the retort of the chemist, and useful truths took their places. One by one religious conceptions have been placed in the crucible of science, and thus far, nothing but dross has been found. A new world has been discovered by the microscope; everywhere has been found the infinite; in every direction man has investigated and explored and nowhere, in earth or stars, has been found the footstep of any being superior to or independent of nature. Nowhere has been discovered the slightest evidence of any interference from without.

These are the sublime truths that enabled man to throw off the yoke of superstition. These are the splendid facts that snatched the sceptre of authority from the hands of priests.

In that vast cemetery, called the past, are most of the religions of men, and there, too, are nearly all their gods. The sacred temples of India were ruins long ago. Over column and cornice; over the painted and pictured walls, cling and creep the trailing vines. Brahma, the golden, with four heads and four arms; Vishnu, the sombre, the punisher of the wicked, with his three eyes, his crescent, and his necklace of skulls; Siva, the destroyer, red with seas of blood; Kali, the goddess; Draupadi, the white-armed, and Chrishna, the Christ, all passed away and left the thrones of heaven desolate. Along the banks of the sacred Nile, Isis no longer wandering weeps, searching for the dead Osiris. The shadow of Typhon's scowl falls no more upon the waves. The sun rises as of yore, and his golden beams still smite the lips of Memnon, but Memnon is as voiceless as the Sphinx. The sacred fanes are lost in desert sands; the dusty mummies are still waiting for the resurrection promised by their priests, and the old beliefs, wrought in curiously sculptured stone, sleep in the mystery of a language lost and dead. Odin, the author of life and soul, Vili and Ve, and the mighty giant Ymir, strode long ago from the icy halls of the North; and Thor, with iron glove and glittering hammer, dashes mountains to the earth no more. Broken are the circles and cromlechs of the ancient Druids; fallen upon the summits of the hills, and covered with the centuries' moss, are the sacred cairns. The divine fires of Persia and of the Aztecs, have died out in the ashes of the past, and there is none to rekindle, and none to feed the holy flames. The harp of Orpheus is still; the drained cup of Bacchus has been thrown aside; Venus lies dead in stone, and her white bosom heaves no more with love. The streams still murmur, but no naiads bathe; the trees still wave, but in the forest aisles no dryads dance. The gods have flown from high Olympus. Not even the beautiful women can lure them back, and Danæ lies unnoticed, naked to the stars. Hushed forever are the thunders of Sinai; lost are the voices of the prophets, and the land once flowing with milk and honey, is but a desert waste. One by one, the myths have faded from the clouds: one by one, the phantom host has disappeared, and one by one, facts, truths and realities have taken their places. The supernatural has almost gone, but the natural remains. The gods have fled, but man is here.

Nations, like individuals, have their periods of youth, of manhood and decay. Religions are the same. The same inexorable destiny awaits them all. The gods created by the nations must perish with their creators. They were created by men, and like men, they must pass away. The deities of one age are the by-words of the next. The religion of our day, and country, is no more exempt from the sneer of the future than the others have been. When India was supreme, Brahma sat upon the world's throne. When the sceptre passed to Egypt, Isis and Osiris received the homage of mankind. Greece, with her fierce valor, swept to empire, and Zeus put on the purple of authority. The earth trembled with the tread of Rome's intrepid sons, and Jove grasped with mailed hand the thunderbolts of heaven. Rome fell, and Christians from her territory, with the red sword of war, carved out the ruling nations of the world, and now Christ sits upon the old throne. Who will be his successor?

Day by day, religious conceptions grow less and less intense. Day by day, the old spirit dies out of book and creed. The burning enthusiasm, the quenchless zeal of the early church have gone, never, never to return. The ceremonies remain, but the ancient faith is fading out of the human heart. The worn-out arguments fail to convince, and denunciations that once blanched the faces of a race, excite in us only derision and disgust. As time rolls on, the miracles grow mean and small, and the evidences our fathers thought conclusive utterly fail to satisfy us. There is an "irrepressible conflict" between religion and science, and they cannot peaceably occupy the same brain nor the same world.

While utterly discarding all creeds, and denying the truth of all religions, there is neither in my heart nor upon my lips a sneer for the hopeful, loving and tender souls who believe that from all this discord will result a perfect harmony; that every evil will in some mysterious way become a good, and that above and over all there is a being who, in some way, will reclaim and glorify every one of the children of men; but for those who heartlessly try to prove that salvation is almost impossible; that damnation is almost certain; that the highway of the universe leads to hell; who fill life with fear and death with horror; who curse the cradle and mock the tomb, it is impossible to entertain other than feelings of pity, contempt and scorn.

Reason, Observation and Experience — the Holy Trinity of Science — have taught us that happiness is the only good; that the time to be happy is now, and the way to be happy is to make others so. This is enough for us. In this belief we are content to live and die. If by any possibility the existence of a power superior to, and independent of, nature shall be demonstrated, there will then be time enough to kneel. Until then, let us stand erect.

Notwithstanding the fact that infidels in all ages have battled for the rights of man, and have at all times been the fearless advocates of liberty and justice, we are constantly charged by the church with tearing down without building again. The church should by this time know that it is utterly impossible to rob men of their opinions. The history of religious persecution fully establishes the fact that the mind necessarily resists and defies every attempt to control it by violence. The mind necessarily clings to old ideas until prepared for the new. The moment we comprehend the truth, all erroneous ideas are of necessity cast aside.

A surgeon once called upon a poor cripple and kindly offered to render him any assistance in his power. The surgeon began to discourse very learnedly upon the nature and origin of disease; of the curative properties of certain medicines; of the advantages of exercise, air and light, and of the various ways in which health and strength could be restored. These remarks were so full of good sense, and discovered so much profound thought and accurate knowledge, that the cripple, becoming thoroughly alarmed, cried out, "Do not, I pray you, take away my crutches. They are my only support, and without them I should be miserable indeed!" "I am not going," said the surgeon, "to take away your crutches. I am going to cure you, and then you will throw the crutches away yourself."

For the vagaries of the clouds the infidels propose to substitute the realities of earth; for superstition, the splendid demonstrations and achievements of science; and for theological tyranny, the chainless liberty of thought.

We do not say that we have discovered all; that our doctrines are the all in all of truth. We know of no end to the development of man. We cannot unravel the infinite complications of matter and force. The history of one monad is as unknown as that of the universe; one drop of water is as wonderful as all the seas; one leaf, as all the forests; and one grain of sand, as all the stars.

We are not endeavoring to chain the future, but to free the present. We are not forging fetters for our children, but we are breaking those our fathers made for us. We are the advocates of inquiry, of investigation and thought. This of itself, is an admission that we are not perfectly satisfied with all our conclusions. Philosophy has not the egotism of faith. While superstition builds walls and creates obstructions, science opens all the highways of thought. We do not pretend to have circumnavigated everything,

THE GODS.

and to have solved all difficulties, but we do believe that it is better to love men than to fear gods; that it is grander and nobler to think and investigate for yourself than to repeat a creed. We are satisfied that there can be but little liberty on earth while men worship a tyrant in heaven. We do not expect to accomplish everything in our day; but we want to do what good we can, and to render all the service possible in the holy cause of human progress. We know that doing away with gods and supernatural persons and powers is not an end. It is a means to an end: the real end being the happiness of man.

Felling forests is not the end of agriculture. Driving pirates from the sea is not all there is of commerce.

We are laying the foundations of the grand temple of the future — not the temple of all the gods, but of all the people — wherein, with appropriate rites, will be celebrated the religion of Humanity. We are doing what little we can to hasten the coming of the day when society shall cease producing millionaires and mendicants — gorged indolence and famished industry — truth in rags, and superstition robed and crowned. We are looking for the time when the useful shall be the honorable; and when REASON, throned upon the world's brain, shall be the King of Kings, and God of Gods.

You're Being Lied To, So Why Not Start Somewhere Else?

Suppressed Science
Deep Politics
Corporate Misbehavior
Alternative Health

Call Us Today & Order A Subscription

NEXUS Magazine
$29.95 / yr, add $16 / yr for Can-
888 909 7474

www.ingramcontent.com/pod-product-compliance
Lightning Source LLC
Chambersburg PA
CBHW031654040426
42453CB00006B/308